Ordnance Survey Ireland

C000259644

Guides to the V

The Wicklow Way

Introduction and text by Michael Fewer

Published by
Ordnance Survey Ireland
Phoenix Park Dublin 2
1998

ISBN number: 1-901496-12-0

Cartography Design and Print origination
by Ordnance Survey Ireland
Printed by Ordnance Survey Ireland

Photography: Ordnance Survey Ireland,
Michael Fewer and Dúchas (The Heritage Service.)

A catalogue record is available for this book
from the British Library

CONTENTS:

Introduction
Ireland's Way Marked Trails

Ireland's first Way-Marked Trail, the Wicklow Way, was inaugurated in 1984, and since then, a total of 16 new cross-country trails have been established around the country, covering a total of 2,440 km. These routes are gateways to a little known, unspoiled Ireland, far from the well known, more popular tourist resorts. The routes, which are all well signposted, use cross country pathways, forestry roads, unfrequented country roads, and mountain tracks, and are designed to take you away from the cities into the wildernesses and magic places of Ireland without having to risk getting lost in hazardous mountain terrain and without having to endure any strenuous climbs.

Because walking is a relatively young sport in Ireland, you will find that most trails are relatively unfrequented, so it is easy, surrounded by towering peaks and deep valleys, to feel a real sense of wilderness and remoteness. Local people you meet along the way have a rare and genuine welcome that can seem somehow jaded where passing tourists are very common.

There is no reason why, with a little planning, even inexperienced walkers or novices of any age cannot, as long as they are reasonably fit, sample and enjoy suitable sections of these routes. Although some are more than 200 km long, it is not necessary to walk an entire route to gain enjoyment from it. The trails are signposted with standard way marks (a yellow arrow and a "walking man" logo) and where necessary, stiles and bridges have been erected. The routes are inspected annually by the National Waymarked Ways Committee of the Department of Tourism, Sport and Recreation, who co-ordinate their upkeep.

The Wicklow Way

The Wicklow Way was planned over a forty year period by the legendary hill-walker, J B Malone, and extends 132 km from the southern suburbs of Dublin city across the Dublin and Wicklow Mountains to end in a tiny county Carlow village, Clonegal.

The Dublin and Wicklow range is the largest highland area in Ireland, and the most extensive surface granite field in Ireland and Britain. It was formed four hundred million years ago when a great flow of molten granite, welling up from under the earth's mantle, created great bulges in the older surface rocks before cooling and solidifying. As the subsequent millenia crept by, the skin of old rock was eroded away by the harsh primordial weather, exposing the rounded domes of granite that make up the mountains of today. Periodic tectonic movement, and later the action of successive glaciations, moulded the range into an east-to-west corrugation of high rounded ridges and deep river valleys, finishing off to the south in a series of gentle hills.

It is across this scenic and often wild landscape that the Wicklow Way meanders, past lakes and farmland, monasteries and forts, and the beautiful valley of Glendalough to reach the lush lowlands of county Carlow. The route reaches its highest point, 630m, at White Hill, and the longest dis-

Pond in Marley Park

tance between accommodation centres is the 22 km between Knockree and Roundwood. Because it is Ireland's first waymarked trail, and because of its proximity to Dublin, the Wicklow Way is probably the most popular of Ireland's walking trails.

Safety in Remote Areas

Irish mountains are not high in European terms, but in combination with the changable nature of Irish weather, can provide plenty of hazards, and should be respected. Although you are never far from a public road on Ireland's way-marked trails, if you are attempting any hill or mountain walking, it is recommended that you:

1. Wear sturdy shoes or boots with good ankle support.

2. Carry a light rucksack with waterproofs, additional warm clothing, and an energy-giving snack. A whistle can be useful to attract attention in an emergency.

3. Never walk alone in remote areas, and always let someone know where you are going and when you should be expected back.

4. Carry a compass and map if you are walking in remote places. If you cannot use these, do not attempt remote stretches if the weather is doubtful.

5. Check weather forecasts before you set out, and plan your walk to suit you capabilities.

Countryside Code

Always show respect for the countryside in all its aspects; remember that it is not only home for many people, but their workplace too. When enjoying your recreation in the country, please:

1. Leave gates as you find them, either open or closed.

2. Avoid damaging fences, hedges and walls when crossing them.

3. Do not take dogs into areas where there are sheep, which means most mountain areas. If you must bring a dog, it should be kept on a lead.

4. If you are camping, remember that fires are prohibited in forestry areas.

5. Leave no litter behind you and do not pollute streams.

Introduction
Les itinéraires de randonnée balisés "Ireland's Way"

Premier itinéraire de randonnée aménagé en Irlande, le "Wicklow Way" a été inaugurée en 1984. Depuis lors, 16 nouveaux itinéraires de cross-country, couvrant un total de 2.240 km, ont été créés dans le pays. Ces itinéraires de randonnée permettent de découvrir une Irlande vierge et peu connue, loin des sentiers battus et des villes touristiques. Ils sont bien balisés et utilisent des chemins de cross-country, des allées forestières, des routes de campagne peu fréquentées et des sentiers de montagne. Ils sont conçus pour vous emmener loin des villes, découvrir la magie de l'Irlande et ses régions sauvages, sans risquer de vous perdre dans les montagnes ni de vous épuiser le long de chemins trop ardus.

La marche étant une activité relativement nouvelle en Irlande, vous constaterez que la plupart de nos itinéraires sont assez peu fréquentés et qu'il est facile au milieu de pics majestueux ou au fond d'une vallée profonde d'éprouver une extraordinaire sensation de dépaysement et de solitude. Les habitants que vous rencontrez en chemin vous accueillent avec une chaleur rare et véritable qui pourrait sembler artificielle dans des régions plus fréquentées par les touristes.

Avec un peu de préparation, et s'ils sont en bonne santé, rien n'interdit aux marcheurs les plus inexpérimentés ou aux novices de tous âges d'essayer certaine sections de ces itinéraires et de les apprécier. Bien que ces itinéraires couvrent parfois plus de 200km, il n'est pas nécessaire de les suivre dans leur totalité pour en profiter. Leur balisage utilise des signes conventionnels courants : flèches jaunes et logo d'un "marcheur". Des ponts et des échaliers ont été aménagés aux emplacements nécessaires. Ces itinéraires sont inspectés tous les ans par le comité national des "Waymarked Ways" qui dépend du ministère du Tourisme, des Sports et des Loisirs et coordonne leur entretien.

Le Wicklow Way

L'élaboration de cet itinéraire a pris une quarantaine d'années au légendaire marcheur J B Malone. Couvrant une distance de 132km entre les faubourgs sud de Dublin et Clonegal, un minuscule village du Comté de Carlow, il traverse les montagnes du Comté de Dublin et du Wicklow.

La chaîne de montagne de Dublin et Wicklow représente la plus vaste région de hautes terres en Irlande, et le plus grand champ de granit d'Irlande et de Grande-Bretagne. Elle s'est formée il y a quatre cent millions d'années lorsqu'un large flot de granit liquide s'accumulant sous le manteau de la terre a créé de grands plis dans les roches plus anciennes de la surface avant de se refroidir et de se solidifier. Avec le passage des millénaires, la roche ancienne soumise àl'érosion du rude climat primordial a exposé les dômes granitiques qui forment les montagnes d'aujourd'hui. Un mouvement tectonique périodique auquel s'est ajoutée plus tard l'action de glaciations successives ont moulé ces montagnes en une succession de plis d'Est en Ouest présentant une alternance de hautes croupes et de profondes vallées fluviales se terminant au sud par une série de collines.

C'est au milieu de ces paysages magnifiques et souvent très sauvages que serpente le Wicklow Way. Longeant des lacs, des terres agricoles, de monastères et de forts, et passant par la très belle vallée de Glendalough, cet itinéraire aboutit dans les basses terres fertiles du Comté de Carlow. Il atteint son point culminant à White Hill (630m), et sa plus longue section entre centres d'hébergement (22km) se trouve entre Knockree et Roundwood. Le fait qu'il ait été le premier itinéraire balisé d'Irlande et sa proximité de Dublin, expliquent probablement la popularité du Wicklow Way.

Consignes de sécurité à respecter

Les montagnes irlandaises ne sont pas très élevées en termes européens mais, dans un pays où le temps change très rapidement, elles peuvent présenter de multiples dangers qu'il ne faut pas sous-estimer. Bien que les itinéraires balisés d'Irlande ne se trouvent jamais à très grande distance d'une route publique, il est conseillé de respecter les consignes suivantes si l'on prévoit une promenade dans les collines ou la montagne:

1. Porter de bonnes chaussures de marche, supportant bien les chevilles

2. Emporter un sac a dos léger contenant des vêtements imperméables, des vêtements chauds supplémentaires et quelques aliments énergétiques. Un sifflet pourra être utile en cas d'urgence.

3. Ne jamais se promener seul dans une région isolée et toujours prévenir quelqu'un avant de partir en indiquant son itinéraire approximatif et l'heure à laquelle on compte rentrer.

4. Se munir d'une boussole et d'une carte si l'on se rend dans un lieu isolé. Si ce n'est pas possible, ne pas tenter de traverser une région isolée lorsque le temps est incertain.

5. S'informer de la météo avant de partir et choisir une promenade correspondant a son niveau.

Le code du randonneur

Respectez l'environnement en toutes circonstances sans oublier qu'il représente pour de nombreuses personnes, non seulement leur lieu d'habitation mais également leur lieu de travail. Lorsque vous vous promenez pour votre plaisir dans la campagne, veuillez respecter les consignes suivantes :

1. Laissez les barrières dans l'état où vous les avez trouvées (ouvertes ou fermées).
2. Évitez d'endommager les clôtures, les haies et les murs lorsque vous les franchissez.
3. N'emmenez jamais un chien aux endroits où il y a des moutons (c'est pratiquement toujours le cas en montagne). Si vous devez emmener votre chien, gardez-le en laisse.
4. Si vous faites du camping, n'oubliez pas que les feux sont interdits en forêt.
5. Ramassez vos ordures avant de partir et ne polluez pas les cours d'eau.

Einführung
Irlands markierte Wanderwege

Der Wicklow-Weg, Irlands erster markierter Wanderweg, wurde 1984 eröffnet. Seither wurden im ganzen Land insgesamt 16 neue Wanderwege mit einer Gesamtlänge von 2.440 km errichtet. Abseits der beliebten und wohlbekannten Fremdenverkehrsgebiete eröffnet sich dem Besucher auf diesen Wanderrouten das unentdeckte, unberührte Irland. Auf gut markierten Pfaden, Waldstraßen, kaum befahrenen Landstraßen und Bergpässen gelangen Sie in die geheimnisvolle und naturbelassene Landschaft Irlands abseits der Städte, ohne dabei Gefahr zu laufen, sich in unwegsamen Gebirgsterrain zu verirren und anstrengende Klettertouren zu unternehmen.

Bergwandern ist ein relativ junger Sport in Irland, und Sie werden feststellen, daß die meisten Wanderpfade nur wenig frequentiert sind, so daß Sie inmitten aufragender Berggipfel und abfallender Täler die naturbelassene Abgeschiedenheit wahrhaftig zu spüren bekommen. Die Einheimischen, die Sie unterwegs treffen, freuen sich noch aufrichtig, Sie zu sehen, ein Gefühl, das sich in den von Touristen frequentierteren Gebieten vielleicht schon eher verloren hat.

Mit etwas Planung können sogar unerfahrene Bergwanderer oder Anfänger aller Altersgruppen geeignete Streckenabschnitte ausprobieren und genießen, vorausgesetzt, sie sind einigermaßen fit. Einige Wanderwege erstrecken sich zwar über 200 km, aber wer sagt denn, daß unbedingt die gesamte Strecke geschafft werden muß? Die Wanderwege sind gut gekennzeichnet - ein Wanderer auf einem gelben pfeilförmigen Schild weist den Weg. Gegebenenfalls wurden Kletterhilfen und Brücken errichtet. Die Wanderwege werden jährlich vom Ausschuß für nationale markierte Wanderwege des Ministeriums für Fremdenverkehr, Sport und Freizeit auf ihre Sicherheit hin überprüft und erhalten.

Der Wicklow-Weg

Der Wicklow-Weg wurde vom legendären Bergwanderer J.B. Malone über einen Zeitraum von mehr als 40 Jahren entworfen, erstreckt sich über 132 km von den südlichen Vororten der Stadt Dublin aus über die Dublin und Wicklow Mountains und endet in dem kleinen Dorf Clonegal in der Grafschaft Carlow.

Die Bergkette der Dublin und Wicklow Mountains ist das größte Hochlandgebiet Irlands und zählt zu den größten Granitregionen Irlands und Großbritanniens. Sie entstand vor vierhundert Millionen Jahren, als ein Fluß aus geschmolzenem Granit aus dem Erdmantel emporquoll und vor seinem Abkühlen und Erstarren riesige Wölbungen am älteren Oberflächengestein hinterließ. Im Laufe des darauffolgenden Jahrtausends wurde die Oberfläche des Altgesteins durch das rauhe Urklima ausgewaschen und setzte die abgerundeten Granitkuppel, welche die Bergkette in ihrem heutigen Erscheinungsbild ausmachen, frei. Periodisch einsetzende Erdbewegungen und die danach aufeinanderfolgenden Stadien der Vergletscherung gestalteten den Gebirgszug zu einer von Osten nach Westen reichenden Bergkette mit hohen abgerundeten Plateaus und tief abfallenden Flußtälern, die im Süden in sanftes Hügelland übergeht.

Durch diese sehenswerte und beizeiten wild anmutende Landschaft schlängelt sich der Wicklow-Weg, vorbei an Seen und Weideland, Klöstern und Forts und dem wunderschönen Tal von Glendalough bis hin zu den üppigen Niederungen der Grafschaft Carlow. Seine höchste Erhebung erreicht man bei White Hill auf einer Seehöhe von 630 m, die weiteste Entfernung von einer Übernachtungsmöglichkeit zur anderen beträgt 22 km zwischen Knockree und Roundwood. Als erster markierter Wanderweg Irlands und aufgrund seiner Nähe zu Dublin zählt der Wicklow-Weg wahrscheinlich zu den beliebtesten Wanderwegen des Landes.

Sicherheit in abgelegenen Regionen

Im Vergleich zu europäischen Gebirgszügen ist die irische Bergwelt zwar nicht hoch, kann aber im Zusammenspiel mit dem wechselhaften irischen Klimas dennoch eine Reihe von Gefahren bergen, die nicht auf die leichte Schulter genommen werden sollten. Obwohl Sie sich auf Irlands Wanderwegen nie allzu weit entfernt von einer öffentlichen Landstraße befinden, sollten Sie bei allen Bergwanderungen oder Klettertouren folgendes beachten:

1. Tragen Sie festes Schuhwerk oder Wanderstiefel.

2. Nehmen Sie wetterfeste und zusätzliche warme Kleidung sowie einen energiespendenden Imbiß in einem leichten Rucksack mit. Eine Pfeife kann sich im Notfall als nützlich erweisen, um auf sich aufmerksam zu machen.

3. Gehen Sie nie alleine in abgelegene Gebiete und teilen Sie immer jemanden mit, wohin Sie gehen und wann Sie beabsichtigen, zurückzukehren.

4. Packen Sie einen Kompaß und eine Wanderkarte ein, wenn Sie sich in abgelegene Gebiete begeben. Wenn Sie mit deren Gebrauch nicht vertraut sind, lassen Sie sich bei Schlechtwetter nicht auf Wanderungen in abgelegenen Streckenabschnitten ein.

5. Achten Sie auf die Wettervorhersage, bevor Sie losgehen, und muten Sie sich bei der Planung Ihrer Wanderung nicht zuviel zu.

Verhaltensregeln in der Natur

Respektieren Sie die Landschaft in all Ihren Gesichtspunkten: Bedenken Sie, daß die hier lebenden Menschen auch hier arbeiten. Wenn Sie auf dem Land Urlaub machen, beachten Sie bitte folgendes:

1. Lassen Sie Gatter in ihrer ursprünglichen Position, entweder geöffnet oder geschlossen.
2. Achten Sie beim Wandern darauf, Zäune, Hecken und Mauern nicht zu beschädigen.
3. Vergessen Sie nicht, daß Hund in jenen Gebieten, in denen sich Schafe befinden - also in praktisch allen Berggebieten - verboten sind. Wenn Sie unbedingt einen Hund mitnehmen müssen, dann führen Sie ihn an einer Leine.
4. Falls Sie ein Zelt aufschlagen, bedenken Sie, daß offenes Feuer in Waldgebieten verboten ist.
5. Lassen Sie keine Abfälle liegen und verschmutzen Sie nicht die Gewässer.

Useful Phone Numbers and Addresses.

EMERGENCY SERVICE   Telephone: 999 or 112
Fire, Gardai, Ambulance, Lifeboat,
Coastal, Mountain and Cave Rescue.

BORD FAILTE (IRISH TOURIST BOARD)
Baggot Street Bridge,
Dublin 2
Telephone: **01 6764764**   Facsimile : **016764764**

WICKLOW COUNTY COUNCIL,
County Buildings
Wicklow
Telephone **0404 67324**

BUS EIREANN, INFORMATION BUREAU,
Travel Centre, Store Street,
Dublin 1;
Telephone: **01 8366111**

IARNROD EIREANN (RAIL PASSENGER INFORMATION)
Connolly Station,
Dublin 1
Telephone: **01 8366222**

ST KEVINS BUS SERVICE
 (serving Roundwood and Glendalough)
 Roundwood,
County Wicklow,
Telephone: **01 281 8119**

AN OIGE (IRISH YOUTH HOSTEL ASSOCIATION)
61 Mountjoy Street,
Dublin 1
Telephone: **01 8304555**   Facsimile: **01 8305808**
INDEPENDANT HOLIDAY HOSTELS,
21 Store Street,
Dublin 1
Telephone : **01 8364710**   Facsimile: **01 8364710**
Email: **ihh@internet_eireann.ie**

DEPARTMENT OF TOURISM, SPORT AND RECREATION
Floor 3, Frederick Buildings
South Frederick Street
Dublin 2
Telephone : **01 6621444**   Facsimile: **01 6799285**

Accommodation along the Way

Although there are not many accommodation possibilities actually on the route, it passes near many villages that can provide a range of facilities from hotels and guesthouses to basic hostel accommodation and camping. Consult with Bord Failte regarding what might be suitable to your needs. Some B&B proprietors are happy to pick you up and drop you off again the following morning, so do enquire.

Bed and Breakfast accommodation is available at:
Enniskerry, Roundwood, Annamoe,
Laragh, Glendalough, Glenmalure,
Aughrim, Tinehely, Shillelagh,
and near Clonegal.

Hostel accomodation is available at:
Knockree, Glencree, Glendalough
and Aghavannagh

Hotel accommodation is available at:
Glencree, Enniskerry, Roundwood,
Glendalough and Aughrim.

Gnéithe ginearálta. General features.
Traits généraux. Signaturen.

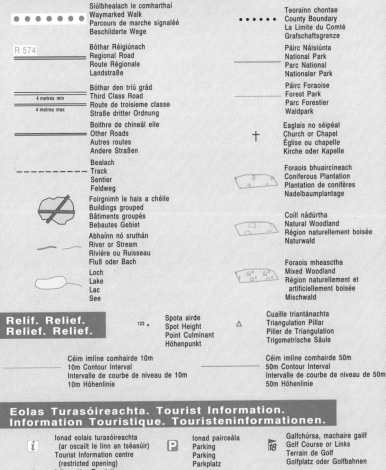

• • • • • • • •
Siúlbhealach le comharthaí
Waymarked Walk
Parcours de marche signaléé
Beschilderte Wege

R 574
Bóthar Réigiúnach
Regional Road
Route Régionale
Landstraße

4 metres min
4 metres max
Bóthar den tríú grád
Third Class Road
Route de troisieme classe
Straße dritter Ordnung

Boithre de cineál eile
Other Roads
Autres routes
Andere Straßen

Bealach
Track
Sentier
Feldweg

Foirgnimh le hais a chéile
Buildings grouped
Bâtiments groupés
Bebautes Gebiet

Abhainn nó sruthán
River or Stream
Rivière ou Ruisseau
Fluß oder Bach

Loch
Lake
Lac
See

Teorainn chontae
County Boundary
La Limite du Comté
Grafschaftsgrenze

Páirc Náisiúnta
National Park
Parc National
Nationaler Park

Páirc Foraoise
Forest Park
Parc Forestier
Waldpark

✝
Eaglais no séipéal
Church or Chapel
Église ou chapelle
Kirche oder Kapelle

Foraois bhuaircíneach
Coniferous Plantation
Plantation de conifères
Nadelbaumplantage

Coill nádúrtha
Natural Woodland
Région naturellement boisée
Naturwald

Foraois mheasctha
Mixed Woodland
Région naturellement et
artificiellement boisée
Mischwald

Relíf. Relief. Relief. Relief.

123 •
Spota airde
Spot Height
Point Culminant
Höhenpunkt

△
Cuaille triantánachta
Triangulation Pillar
Pilier de Triangulation
Trigometrische Säule

Céim imlíne comhairde 10m
10m Contour Interval
Intervalle de courbe de niveau de 10m
10m Höhenlinie

Céim imlíne comhairde 50m
50m Contour Interval
Intervalle de courbe de niveau de 50m
50m Höhenlinie

Eolas Turasóireachta. Tourist Information.
Information Touristique. Touristeninformationen.

ℹ️
Ionad eolais turasóireachta
(ar oscailt le linn an tséasúir)
Tourist Information centre
(restricted opening)
Information Touristique
(ouverture limitée)
Touristeninformation
(beschränkte Öffnungszeiten)

P
Ionad pairceála
Parking
Parking
Parkplatz

18
Galfchúrsa, machaire gailf
Golf Course or Links
Terrain de Golf
Golfplatz oder Golfbahnen

Láithreán picnící
Picnic site
Ères de Pique-nique
Picknickplatz

•
Séadchomhartha Ainmnithe
Named Antiquities
Monuments mentionnes
Namentlich aufgeführte
Altetümer

▲ Ⓐ
Brú An Óige / Neamhspleách
Hostel An Óige / Independent
Auberge An Óige / Indépendant
Herberge An Óige / Unabhängig

☀️
Ionad dearctha
Viewpoint
Point de vue
Aussichtspunkt

○
Clós, m.sh. Ráth nó Lios
Enclosure, e.g. Ringfort
Enceinte fortifice
Einfriedung, z.B. Ringfort

PO
Oifig phoist
Post office
Bureau de Poste
Post

☎
Teilefón Poiblí
Public Telephone
Cabine Téléphonique
Telefonzelle

🍺
Tábhairne
Public House
Auerge
Gasthaus

SCÁLA 1:25 000 SCALE 1:25 000

0.5 KILOMETRES   0   1   2 KILOMETRES

1/2 STATUTE MILE   0   1 STATUTE MILE

4 ceintiméadar sa chiliméadar (taobh chearnóg eangaí)
4 centimetres to 1 Kilometre (grid square side)

The Wicklow Way

The Wicklow Way begins beside Marlay House, built around 1794 by the Dublin banking, family the La Touches. They were a very influential family at the time; apart from counting four Members of Parliament among their number, they were connected by marriage to Henry Grattan, the major Irish statesman and political orator of the day. When Marlay House was built, the 160 hectare demesne was extensively landscaped with more than 300 varieties of trees and shrubs being planted, and the Little Dargle River, a mountain brook which flowed through the land, being harnessed into a series of waterfalls and small lakes. Today the Marlay demesne is a popular public park.

South of Marlay Park is St Columba's College, founded in 1843 and once considered the Eton of Ireland. In 1896 a fire broke out in one of the buildings, and boys had to escape by making ropes out of sheets. The fire brigade was four hours late, but the rest of the school was saved when the wind direction changed at the last minute! A plaque commemorating this kind Zephyr can be seen today on the cloisters wall.

The route climbs towards the mountains past the ruins of a school and a woolen mill, and leaves the public road at Kilmashoge Wood carpark. South of the carpark, in a glade in the wood, are a pair of megalithic tombs, the oldest a gallery grave dating from the Neolithic period. The later tomb, built in the Bronze Age 1,500 years later, is a small cist grave resembling a stone-lined box.

Three Rock Mountain

It was constructed from slabs taken from the earlier tomb, an early example of vandalism! The tombs were excavated in 1953, bringing to light some fine Bronze Age food vessels.

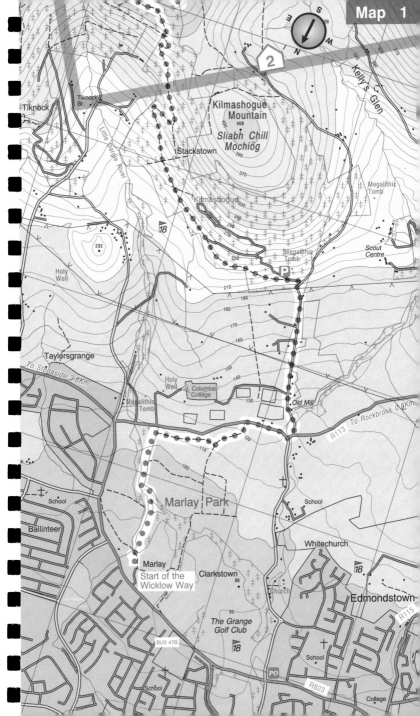

Map 1

The Wicklow Way continues to ascend the eastern slopes of Kilmashoge, the nearest of the Dublin mountains to the city. It was originally covered with a layer of blanket bog, which, due to its proximity to the city, was stripped away as it was harvested for fuel during the last few centuries. Archaeologists have recently discovered a network of agricultural field walls covering the flat-topped summit, that were exposed when the peat was cut away. As the original peat began to grow on this mountain around the middle of the Neolithic time, it is thought that these field divisions date from that time, and that the stone-age people who built the passage grave near the Kilmashoge Wood carpark (see page 16) farmed this and adjacent hilltops.

The route leaves the forestry road and climbs towards the south onto open moorland. Nearby is the Fairy Castle, a cairn of stones that probably covers another pre-historic grave. There is a concentration of these hilltop cairns in the Dublin mountains and further south in the Wicklow mountains, suggesting that in the Neolithic and early Bronze Age period the area had a substantial population.

The route descends into Glendhu (The Dark Glen), the first of a series of east-west valleys to be crossed on the Wicklow Way. About 2km to the left when the route reaches the road is the old quarry worker's hamlet of Glencullen, where you will find a public house called Foxes, said to be the highest in Ireland.

In the woods above the hamlet of Boranaraltry keep an eye out for your first glimpse of deer on the Wicklow Way. The main two species in Wicklow are the native red deer and the imported sika deer, but these two species have interbred so much it is not clear if any pure reds remain.

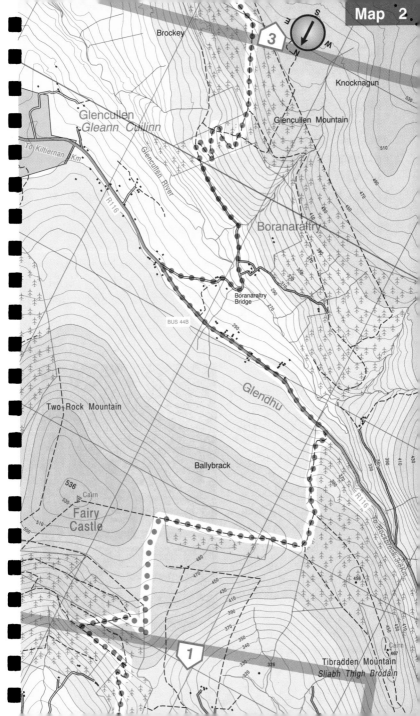

Map 2

The route takes you over the next range, Glencullen Mountain, near the 555m summit called Prince William's Seat, named after a visit of the prince when he came to Ireland with his father, George IV, in 1821.

The next valley to be crossed is Glencree Valley, which was established in the 13th century as a Royal Deerpark, and stocked with eighty red deer sent from the royal forest at Chester in England. The valley was at the time covered, as was most of Wicklow, with a primeval oak forest , and an embankment was built around the park to prevent the deer escaping into the wild, where the native Irish would quickly benefit from them. It was a serious crime to poach the King's deer; records show however that the Abbot of the powerful St Mary's Abbey in Dublin was one of those caught in the act, 'with nets and other engines and greyhounds' that lived to tell the tale!

The original oak woods in Glencree suffered the same fate as the rest of the Irish wildwood. At the end of the 13th century a timber works was established in the valley to provide wood for the erection of a castle in Haverford in Wales for Queen Eleanor, wife of King Edward I subsequently Wicklow oak was exported in vast quantities for construction and for shipbuilding, and within a few centuries, all but some small fragments of the original oakwoods had disappeared.

Miners Road

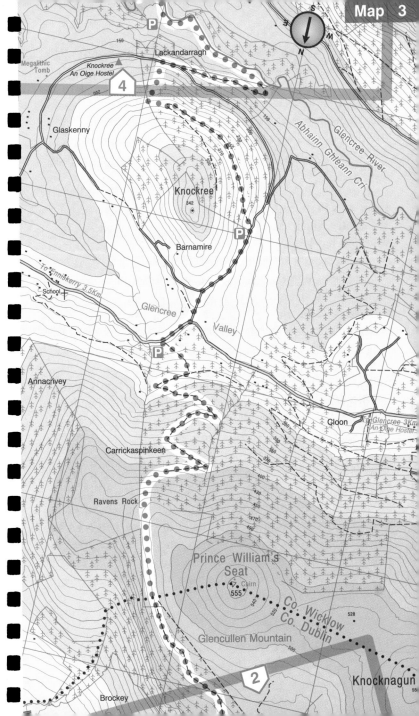

Map 3

P

Lackandarragh

Knockree
An Óige Hostel

4

Megalithic
Tomb

Glaskenny

Knockree

342

Barnamire

P

To Enniskerry 3.5Km

School

Glencree

Valley

Abhainn Ghleann Crí

Glencree River

P

Annacrivey

Cloon

Glencree 3Km
An Óige Hostel

Carrickaspinkeen

Ravens Rock

Prince William's
Seat

Cairn
555

Co. Wicklow
Co. Dublin

528

Glencullen Mountain

2

Brockey

Knocknagun

Crossing the Glencree River, the route ascends through coniferous forest to reach a high pathway that promenades around the Powerscourt Deerpark. The district of Powerscourt takes its name from the De La Poer family, who came into possession of the lands through marriage with a daughter of the Earl of Pembroke, also known as Strongbow, who pioneered the Norman invasion of Ireland in the 12th century.

From the high path there is a fine view of Powerscourt Waterfall, which cascades 250m into the deerpark. The waterfall has been a tourist attraction since it was described by Arthur Young in his travelogue Tour of Ireland in 1780. When King George IV visited Ireland in 1821, he was entertained to a banquet by Lord Powerscourt at nearby Powerscourt House. A special viewing bridge had been erected across the Dargle River in the deerpark so that the king could view the waterfall, and the river was dammed high above the cascade, so that it could be released spectacularly. Fortunately for the king, he had to depart early before the display; when the torrent was released and it thundered over the cliff and down into the deerpark, it swept the viewing bridge completely away!

After descending through trees, the route comes out of the forest to cross the remains of the old deerpark wall into the broad and peaceful moorland of Glensoulan. Before Ireland's Great Famine in the 1840s this area had a small population of cottiers, and in wintertime, when the bracken is low, the shapes of the remains of their dwellings can be made out, together with faint traces of cultivation ridges extending up the mountain slopes.

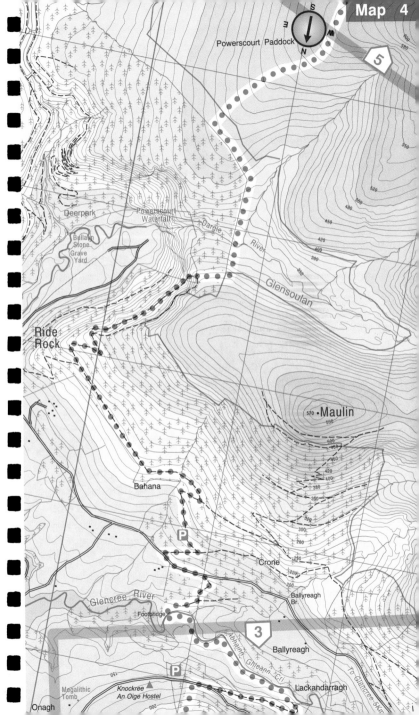

Map 4

5

Powerscourt Paddock

S
E · W
N

Deerpark

Powerscourt
Waterfall

Dargle

River

Glensoulan

Ballawn
Stone
Grave
Yard

Ride
Rock

570 •Maulin

500
490
480
470
460
450
420
400
380
350
320
300
260

Bahana

P

290

Crone

220

200

Ballyreagh
Br.

Glencree River

Footbridge

3

Abhainn Ghleann Cri

Ballyreagh

P

To Glencree 5Km

Megalithic
Tomb

Knockree
An Oige Hostel

Lackandarragh

Onagh

The Wicklow Way now climbs to contour along the eastern slopes of Djouce Mountain. In clear weather the mountains of Wales, although 112km away across the Irish Sea, can be seen from here, the most prominent being the highest summit in Wales, Mount Snowdon.

Near Djouce

Near here, a French Navy Junkers 52 aircraft bringing 22 French Girl Guides to a holiday in Ireland crashed in foggy conditions in August 1946. Boggy ground and the skill of the pilot saved the plane from complete destruction, and all the passengers and crew survived. Over the following months, the remains of the aircraft were taken away by souvenirs hunters and local farmers and up to recently the tailplane and pieces of the characteristic corrugated aluminium sheeting from the fuselage and wings could be identified in the area in use as gates or reinforcing field walls.

The route descends over White Hill, so-called because of its outcrops of glistening quartz and schist , and drops down past a memorial to J. B. Malone, a pioneer of Irish hill-walking and the founder of the Wicklow Way. To the south now is one of the finest vistas of the route, layer after layer of rounded granite mountains, while in the middle distance, up along the green Clohoge valley, Lough Dan, Wicklow's largest natural lake, darkly gleams. To the west Fancy Mountain towers 200m over scenic Lough Tay, which has a picturesque crescent of sandy beach along its north shore.

Concealed under the shoulder of the north-east side of the valley is Luggala Lodge, a beautiful villa built as a hunting lodge by the La Touche family in the late 18th century.

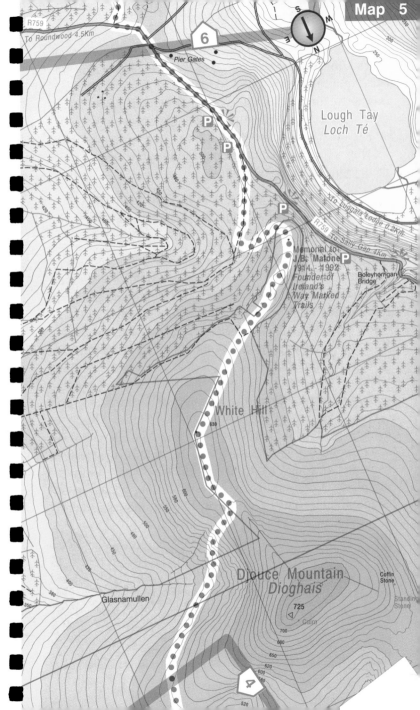

Map 5

S N W E

6

To Roundwood 4.5Km

R759

Pier Gates

Lough Tay
Loch Té

P

P

P

To Luggala Lodge 0.2Km

R759 To Sally Gap 4Km

P

Memorial to
J.B. Malone
1914 - 1992
Founder of
Ireland's
Way Marked
Trails

Boleyhorrigan
Bridge

White Hill

630

600

550

500

450

400

350

400

450

Glasnamullen

Diouce Mountain
Dioghais

Coffin
Stone

Standing
Stone

725
Carn

700

680

650

620

600

580

520

4

The Wicklow Way leaves the public road to enter Sleamaine Forest, from where there are views south-south east along the coast in clear weather to Wicklow Head, with its tall lighthouse. Nearby' to the east' is Vartry Reservoir, a pair of man-made lakes on the Vartry river, the first of which was constructed in 1862 to provide water for the expanding city of Dublin. The facility provides 80 million gallons of water daily to the city and its suburbs.

To the south-west the ragged ridge of Scarr Mountain can be seen, with a backdrop of rounded Tonelegee, Wicklow's third highest mountain at 817m.

The Wicklow Way meanders through the forest, and looping around to give a view of Lough Dan, winds down to the public road again. At this point you are a little more than 2km from Roundwood, which at 238m above sea level boasts of being Ireland's highest village. The fact that walking in Wicklow is not a new phenomenon is evidenced by the comment in Wright's Guide of 1822 that Roundwood 'affords tolerable accommodation to a party of walkers but the premises are not sufficiently extensive for parties attended by servants and travelling equipages'. Blacks Guide to Wicklow of 1868 mentions that Bed and Breakfast in Roundwood will cost 2s10d (18p), but that it was 'a small hamlet possessing little to interest the tourist save as a resting place'. Today Roundwood is a bustling village with a country market and a good supply of pubs and restaurants.

Luggala or Fancy Mountain

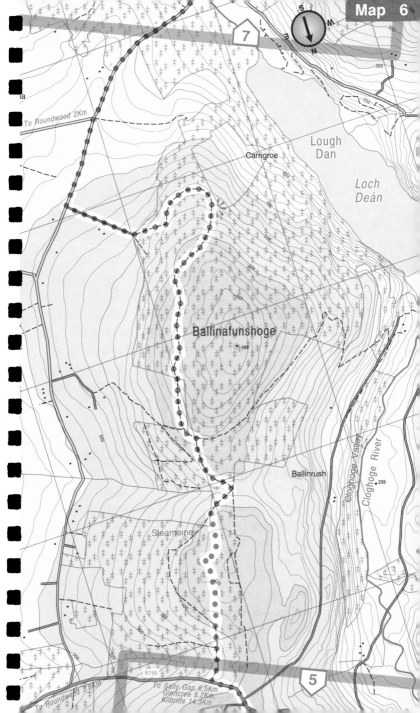

Map 6

7

Lough
Dan

*Loch
Deán*

Carrigroe

Ballinafunshoge

• 480

Ballinrush

Cloghoge Valley

Cloghoge River

• 209

Steamaine

To Roundwood 2Km

To Roundwood 3.8Km

R759

To Sally Gap 6.5Km
Glencree 8.2Km
Kilbride 14.3Km

5

After passing through a remaining fragment of Wicklow's ancient oakwoods, the Avonmore river, flowing out of Lough Dan, is crossed at Oldbridge. A plaque on the bridge states that it was built in 1934, but as the name suggests, it was not the first bridge to be built here. The road is part of an old highway, and before that it was an ancient pack-route; the earliest bridge was probably a wooden one erected to assist monks, pilgrims and journeymen travelling between the monastic settlements at Glendalough, Clondalkin and Tallaght in early Christian times, so as you walk here you walk in the company of the shades of long ago.

At Oldbridge Cross are the back gates of Glendalough House, originally the home of the Bartons, popular Wicklow landowners. The last of the Bartons to live here was Robert Barton, who died in 1976. He was the last surviving member of the delegation who signed the Anglo-Irish Treaty in London in 1921, thus bringing an end to English rule in 26 counties of Ireland. Sickened by the subsequent political chaos that led to the Civil War, he turned his back on politics in 1927 and returned to farm his lands here in Wicklow. Erskine Childers, author of the early 20th century spy thriller 'Riddle of the Sands', also lived here for a time. Although an Englishman, he was a central figure in the importation of the arms that were to be used in the Rebellion of 1916. He was arrested here by the Free State army during the Civil War. Found to be in the possession of a small handgun which had been given to him before the Civil War by Michael Collins, the commander-in-chief of the army, he was executed shortly afterwards.

Leaving the road, the route climbs onto Paddock Hill, scattered with granite boulders deposited there by the last glaciation.

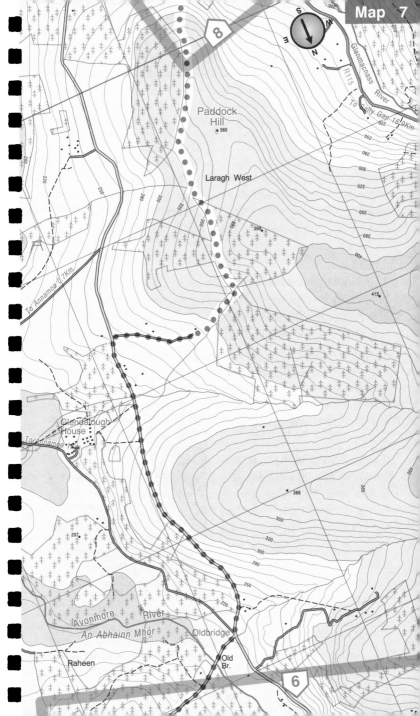

Map 7

8

S

W

E

N

Glenmacnass River

R115

To Sally Gap 16.9 Km

Paddock
Hill
● 360

Laragh West

399 ●

413 ●

To Annamoe 0.7 Km

Glendalough
House

To Annamoe

366 ●

207 ●

Avonmore River

An Abhainn Mhór

Oldbridge

Old
Br.

Raheen

6

The Wicklow Way drops down from Paddock Hill, crosses the Military Road and then a timber footbridge over the Glenmacnass river. A path and a forestry road take you up onto a spur of Brochagh Mountain, where, emerging from the trees, you climb steeply up a rough track over pavements of schist. At the highest point a wonderful vista opens up ahead of the Vale of Glendalough with it's two lakes nestling in the shelter of rounded Camaderry mountain to the north and Derrybawn to the south. The grey shape of the medieval round tower of Glendalough can be seen reaching towards the sky from the midst of the ancient monastic settlement in the valley.

The route drops down through forestry, and after crossing the Wicklow Gap road, a short and narrow boreen takes you down into the hamlet of Glendalough opposite the Royal Hotel, which has been providing accommodation for visitors and pilgrims for over two hundred years. Follow the Way through the Visitor centre and across the Glendasan River, in medieval times the entire valley was thickly clothed in a primeval wildwood of oaks, holly, birch and rowan. Over the centuries these trees gradually disapp- eared as land was cleared for agriculture and timber was harvested for building, fuel and the manufacture of charcoal. A small area of the original native woodland survives on the cliffs along the track which the Wicklow Way follows west- wards past Lower Lake (Loch Péist), the Lake of the Monster.

Bridge over
Glenmacnass River

Map 8

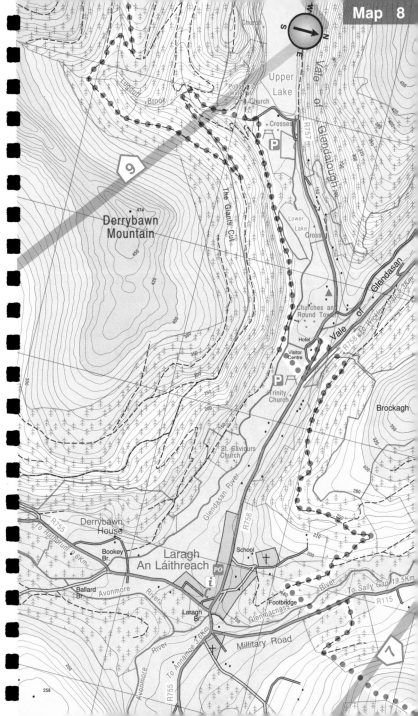

Church

Upper Lake

Vale of Glendalough

Pollanass Waterfall

Church

Crosses

P

R757

The Giant's Cut

Lugduff Brook

9

•474
Derrybawn
Mountain
450

Lower Lake
Cross

Churches and
Round Tower

Hotel

Visitor Centre

P

Trinity Church

St. Saviours Church

Glendasan River

Vale of Glendasan

To Wicklow Gap 5.5Km

R756

Brockagh

R756

R755
To Rathdrum 8.6Km

Derrybawn House

Bookey Br.

Laragh
An Láithreach

PO

i

School

Glenmacnass River

To Sally Gap 19.5Km

R115

Ballard Br.

Avonmore River

Footbridge

Laragh Br.

To Annamoe 5.6Km

Avonmore River

Military Road

R755

258

The Wicklow Way passes by the monastic buildings on the far side of the Glenealo river and continues south-westwards, before turning uphill beside a mountain stream. The fast-flowing cascade has cut a deep gorge in the soft mica schist bedrock, drilling and scooping out pools under the force of its waterfalls. Since the glaciers that carved this landscape receded 10,000 years ago, this little stream has borne more than 20 million tonnes of rock, sand and mud down into the valley, dividing what was originally one lake into two.

The route rises through mixed woodland which includes some sessile oaks, descendants of the trees which covered these hills at the time that St Kevin came to Glendalough. The mountain on the far side of the valley is called Camaderry, which means 'the bend or curve of the oak-wood', harking back to those times. There are very few young oaks growing in the forest now, partly because they are grazed by deer and feral goats that roam the valley, so the species may eventually die out here.

The route follows forestry roads that wind and climb south-wards into remote territory, and then via firebreaks to cross open moorland just below Mullacor at 657m. It is a broad, flat and boggy top, with extensive views to all compass points. To the north-north-west the plateau-topped Turlough Hill cannot be mistaken; the summit contains a reservoir which can be emptied into a set of turbines deep in the mountain to produce electricity when the demand is high on the national grid. The water is pumped back up when demand is low. To the west- south-west, 6km away, is Lugnaquillia, at 925m, Wicklow's highest peak.

Contouring along the southern slopes of Mullacor, the route descends into the deep valley of Glenmalure. It is a broad U-shaped valley, gouged out of the granite mountains by an ancient glacier, which, as it melted and began to recede, deposited a flat floor of gravel. The Avonbeg river that meanders along the valley is all that remains today of this great glacier.

Glenmalure was for centuries the homeland of the Wicklow clan, the O'Byrnes, and Fiach McHugh O'Byrne, leader of the clan in the late 16th century was a thorn in the side of the English. Here in the fastnesses of Wicklow, O'Byrne resisted their rule and maintained Irish customs and laws that had been banished elsewhere. The 'Pale', that zone around Dublin where English law prevailed, constantly suffered raids by his men for livestock, arms and other commodities that were difficult to obtain in the mountains; in one such foray the roof of the church of Crumlin in south Dublin was relieved of its lead because the rebels were running out of shot!

In 1580 Queen Elizabeth I gave Lord Winton de Grey the task of finally putting to an end to O'Byrne. He led a large force into Glenmalure from the western end hoping to surprise the chieftain, but the English were led into a classic ambush, and defeated. Eight hundred soldiers were said to have died in the battle, which ended when Lord Grey fled westwards leaving behind his caravan of belongings; it is said that a young Walter Raleigh and the poet Edmund Spencer were amongst those who also escaped. It was almost twenty years before government forces again ventured deep into the mountains.

Crossing the Avonbeg river, the route passes the remains of the old military barracks, built about 1800, and ascends into Drumgoff Wood.

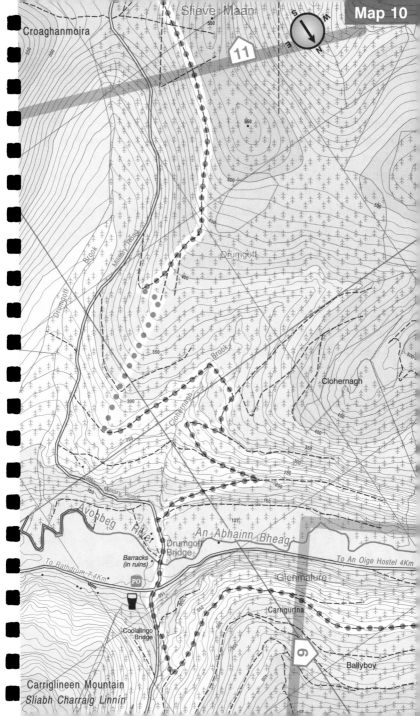

Following a forestry road that passes to the east of Slieve Maan, the route drops down to the public road for a short distance. This is the Military Road, built by the English a few years after the 1798 rebellion. For centuries, the Wicklow mountains had provided sanctuary for the rebellious Irish, and never more so than during that uprising, when rebels like General Holt and the legendary Michael Dwyer carried on a guerilla war here in Wicklow against the forces of the crown. Dwyer remained at large for nearly three years after the rebellion had been put down, leading a charmed life and escaping capture many times. He gave himself up to the authorities in 1800, and they were so relieved to be spared further years of his rebel activities that they agreed to commute his death sentence and instead to transport him with his family to Botany Bay in Australia. The Dwyers settled comfortably into the new colony and the erst-while Irish rebel became a pillar of the community there, reaching the rank of Constable before his death in 1825.

The Military Road was built to allow the speedy deployment of the army out of barracks in Dublin 50km into the heart of Wicklow, and it sounded the death-knell for the rebel's mountain sanctuary. Strong fortified barracks, the remains of one of which was passed at Glenmalure, were built at regular intervals along the road. Two of the barracks survive intact today, one at Glencree as a Centre for Peace and Reconciliation, and another at Aughavannagh, up to recently a Youth Hostel.

The Wicklow Way contours around Carrickashane mountain from which there are fine views north-north-west up the valley of the Ow river to the cliffs of Lugnaquillia, Wicklow's highest mountain. The route descends to cross the Ow by way of a picturesque iron bridge.

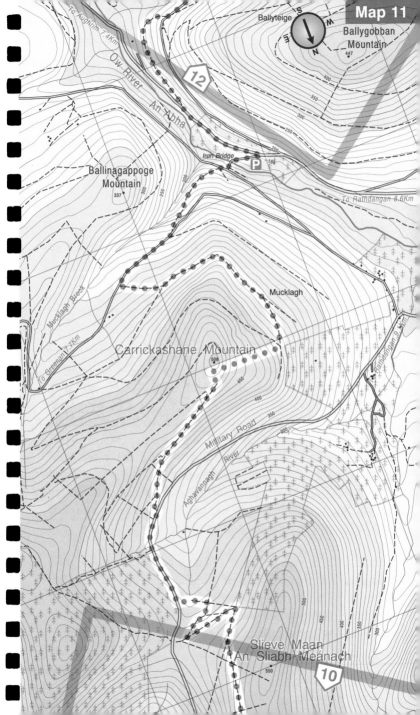

A change in the general topography of the surrounding landscape is apparent as the route makes its way farther south; the higher and more dramatic mountains have been left behind north of Glenmalure, and in their place are a series of rounded granite hills leading south-west in a narrow band. Many of these hills are covered with recent coniferous plantations; almost 19% of the county of Wicklow is under forest, which makes it one of Ireland's most heavily afforested areas. Most of this planting has taken place since 1960, and currently there are concerns that this concentration on monocultures of conifers may ultimately prove harmful. Research in the USA and Europe has shown that plantations of conifers on poor soils pollute the streams draining the areas, leading to a broad range of problems downstream, and these effects are being monitored in Wicklow today.

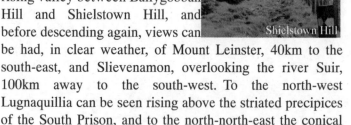

Shielstown Hill

The Wicklow Way ascends a rising valley between Ballygobban Hill and Shielstown Hill, and before descending again, views can be had, in clear weather, of Mount Leinster, 40km to the south-east, and Slievenamon, overlooking the river Suir, 100km away to the south-west. To the north-west Lugnaquillia can be seen rising above the striated precipices of the South Prison, and to the north-north-east the conical top of Croghanmoira can be identified.

Local people still retain the memory of a tragedy that occurred on the far side of Shielstown Hill in the 19th century. After a heavy snowfall, young people enjoying a snowball fight started an avalanche which swept away a cottage in which a farmer, his wife and four children died.

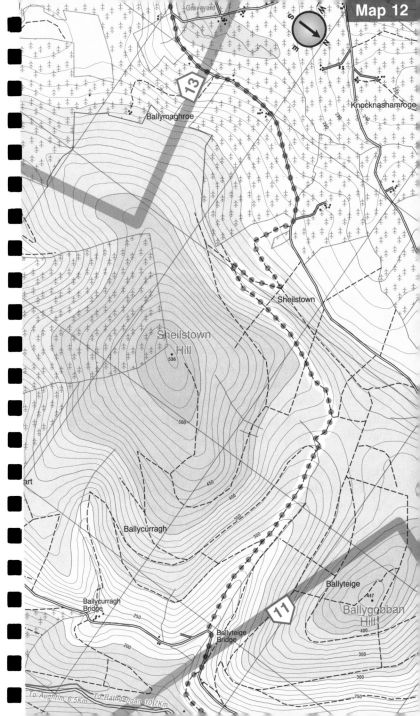

Map 12

Graveyard

Knocknashamroge

13

Ballymaghroe

Sheilstown

Sheilstown
Hill

536

500

450

400

300

250

200

Ballycurragh

300

Ballyteige

Ballygobban
Hill

447

400

350

300

250

Ballycurragh
Bridge

250

Ballyteige
Bridge

11

200

To Aughrim 6.5Km   To Rathdangan 10.7Km

The Wicklow Way winds southwards, passing near the pretty stone-built hamlet of Moyne. The hamlet's centrepiece is a fine, granite-built First Fruits church which overlooks one of the earliest National Schools established in Ireland, built in 1822 to cater for as many as eighty boys and girls. The building is now a pretty dwelling house. The name 'Moyne' is an old one and predates the hamlet - it comes from the Gaelic for 'morass', probably because the surrounding land- scape is mostly bog and moorland.

East of Moyne the route briefly follows a narrow track down-hill: on the right at the junction with another tarmac road, near a new bungalow, are the remains of a holy well dedicat-ed to St Colmcille. In ancient Ireland certain spring wells were regarded as emanating from the underworld, and there-fore possessed magical properties. During the early Christian period, many of the pagan beliefs were absorbed into the new faith, and magical wells such as this became Christianised, often named by a passing saint who blessed them. Colmcille was one of the most important of Ireland's early Christian saints, and he founded monasteries all over Ireland before travelling to the Scottish island of Iona and converting the people of Scotland.

Crossing a stream over a narrow bridge at a place called Sandy Ford, the name harking back to a time when there was no bridge, the Wicklow Way follows a narrow road as it con-tours around Ballycumber Hill. Soon the dappled slopes of Croghan Kinsella comes into view east-south-east. This mountain was, for a brief time in the 1790s, the site of a fren-zied Gold Rush, following the discovery of large nuggets of gold in the streams flowing off the mountain. Some of the scars left by open-cast mining on the mountain can still be identified from Ballycumber.

Map 13

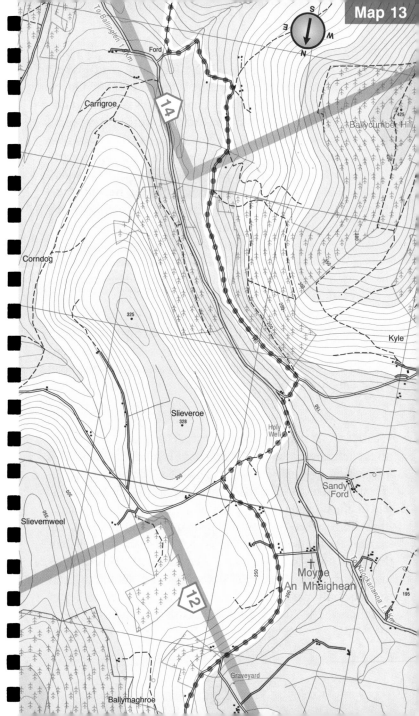

Fording a tiny stream, the route now takes you steeply uphill along an overgrown boreen (Gaelic for 'small road') which in springtime is decorated with bluebells and orchids. Out on the open eastern slopes of Garryhoe hill, look out a short distance uphill for a low bank of earth on which a few small trees are growing. The local name for this is Raheen, which means 'the little rath', and it is what remains of an early Christian farmstead, of a type that is unique to Ireland. About 20,000 of these raths survive all over Ireland, symbolising the rural nature of the country's population in the first millenium AD. A circular ditch and earthen bank, on which there would have been a pallisade or a thick thorn hedge, protected an inner corral for animals and the original homestead, probably a timber framed thatched building.

Further on, mounted on the wall to the left is a memorial stone cross erected in memory of a man who was killed in a shooting accident here in the early 1900s. The route loops around to meet Coolafunshoge Lane, an old droving road from which there are great views across the lush Wicklow lowlands.

The Derry river is crossed before reaching the R747: 1.5km to the left now is the late Georgian village of Tinahely. This place was originally part of the vast estates belonging to Thomas Wentworth, Lord Deputy for Ireland in the 1630s. He had just begun the erection of a great house just outside the village when he was recalled to England in 1639; the remains of the house, which had only reached ground floor level, is known locally as Black Tom's Cellars. Tinahely was burnt down during the 1798 rebellion and the village was subsequently completely re-built by the local landowner of the time, the second Earl Fitzwilliam.

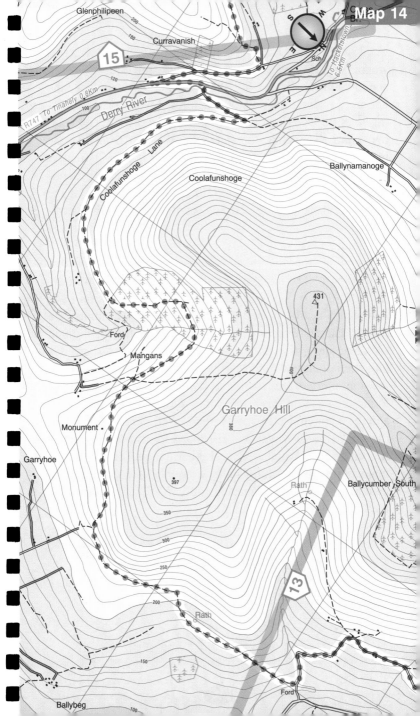

Map 14

Glenphilipeen

Curravanish

15

Sch

To Hacketstown 6·6Km

R747 To Tinahely 0.8Km

Derry River

Coolafunshoge Lane

Coolafunshoge

Ballynamanoge

431

Ford

Mangans

Garryhoe Hill

Monument

Garryhoe

397

Rath

Ballycumber South

350

300

250

13

200

Rath

150

Ford

Ballybeg

100

The Wicklow Way turns onto an often-overgrown boreen that wanders up the western slopes of Muskeagh Hill. The substantial stone walls that line the boreen in places indicate the antiquity of the route, which was probably an ancient droving road for bringing cattle to market. As the boreen meanders along the hillside, there are extensive views out over the lush plains of county Carlow, here only a few kilometres away. Seskin Hill with its twin summits can be easily identified to the west, while Eagle Hill, which rises south of the Carlow village of Hacketstown, can be seen to the northwest.

Descending from the hillside the route passes the hamlet of Mullinacuff. The name is derived from the Gaelic meaning 'McDuff's Mill', and there are possible traces of a mill site and a rath nearby beside the stream that flows though the place. There are records of a number of such watermills in the area, and a few kilometres away to the south there is a holy well dedicated to St Martin. It is tradition in Ireland that the saint met his death by being crushed by a mill-wheel, and to get the saint on their side, some millers named the spring serving their mill-races St Martin's Well, and in honour of the saint all mill-wheels were stopped for a short time on St Martin's day, November 11th. Like Moyne further north, the main buildings in Mullinacuff, a couple of cottages and a gem of a neo-gothic, pinnacled church with lattice windows, are built from Wicklow Granite.

After Stranakelly Cross Roads the Wicklow Way climbs along the northern flanks of Cronelea Hill.

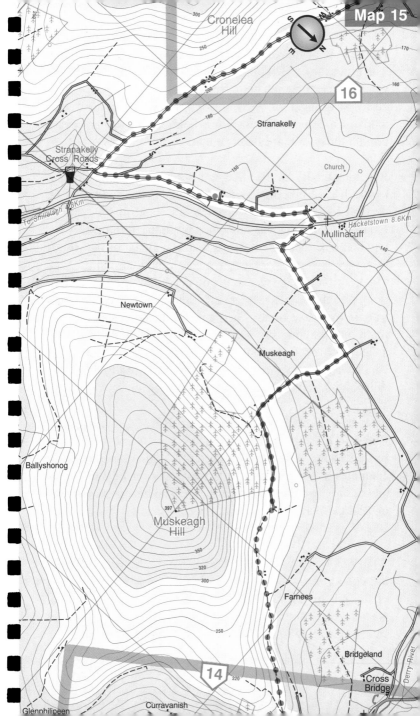

Map 15

Cronelea
Hill

16

Stranakelly

Stranakelly
Cross Roads

Church

To Shillelagh 7.8Km

Hacketstown 8.6Km

Mullinacuff

Newtown

Muskeagh

Ballyshonog

397

Muskeagh
Hill

Farnees

Bridgeland

14

Cross
Bridge

Glennhilipeen

Curravanish

Derry River

As the road begins to descend from Cronelea Hill the church and graveyard at Kilquiggin come into view ahead. There was an ancient church here that was said to have been founded by St Comgan of Wexford; only the very damaged remnants of a celtic high cross in a field east of the graveyard remain today of that establishment.

Reaching the R725, the village of Shillelagh is less than 4km to the left. The name is a very ancient one, and may be derived from the Gaelic meaning 'the land of the tribe of Ealaigh'. The area was renowned up to the 17th century for its great oakwood, the last substantial remnant of the woods that once covered Wicklow, which are now no more. Like Tinahely, the village was in the ownership of the Fitzwilliam family up to the late 19th century, and the stone estate houses date from that time. The name 'shillelagh', given to the traditional walking stick-cum-cudgel, probably derives from a late 18th century song called 'The Sprig of Shillelagh' which was written about the stump of an old oak tree near the village, said to be the last tree of the great forest.

Less than 5km to the right at the R725 can be found Rathgall, the fort of the foreigner, a great stone-walled hill fort enclosing an area of 7.2 hectares. While there are many examples of similar stone forts in the west of Ireland, this is one of only two on the east coast: archaeological excavations of Rathgall have shown it was occupied as far back as 700 BC.

The Wicklow Way crosses the R725 and follows a side road through an area called Boley, which suggests that the summit of the hill to the south was a 'booley', a summer pasture, where in ancient times, young people of a community would camp out for the summer months, tending herds of cattle.

Map 16

17

Barnacashel
319

Mungacullin

300

280

Boley

250

220

200

Boley
Br

150

R725 *To Tullow 10.2Km*

To Shillelagh 2.5Km

Quigginroe

200

Ballymarroge

144

School

Graveyard

Cronelea

Cross

Kilquiggin

150

180

200

Cronelea
Hill

357

300

250

Laragh

15

300

200

180

170

160

After climbing very steeply up a narrow tarmac road, the route turns into forestry at a place called Raheenakit, 'the fort of the cat', recalling a time before wildcats became extinct in Ireland. Out in the open again, an old disused drovers road is followed along the eastern slopes of the hill, with broad views over the fertile farmlands of county Carlow and the valley of the river Barrow. The prominent nearby hill to the south is Gibbet Hill (325m) in county Wexford, the border of which is now less than 7km away, while the Blackstairs Mountains dominate the horizon.

The Wicklow Way continues westwards on a narrow tarmac road; less than 2km to the north at Aghowle ('the field of apple trees') are the well-preserved remains of an early 12th century church, site of an earlier monastery founded by the celebrated St Finian of Clonard. Erected on an ancient prominence of pagan origin, the roofless building has a fine trabeated doorway and tiny Romanesque windows, and near the doorway is a 3.5m-high stone-carved celtic cross.

After founding the church here, St Finian went on to Clonard in county Meath where he established a major monastic settlement. It is said that he missed the sound of his bell at Aghowle so much that he had it brought to Clonard, but it magically returned to Aghowle. Three times it was brought back to Clonard, and chained in place, but each time it returned here to the church in the valley, so Finian finally got the message and left it be!

The route leaves the tarmac road to enter the forestry that covers the west of Moylisha Hill.

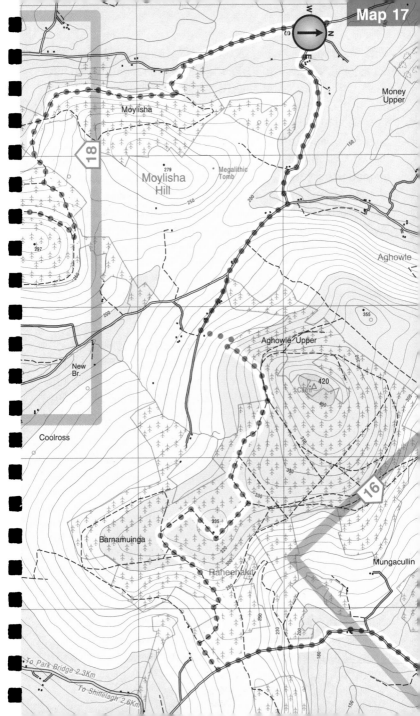

Map 17

Money
Upper

Moylisha

Megalithic
Tomb

Moylisha
Hill

•279

250

200

150

Aghowle

•297

•355

200

Aghowle Upper

New
Br.

420

400

300

Coolross

350

330

16

335

300

Barnamuinga

330

Raheenakit

Mungacullin

250

230

200

180

To Park Bridge 2.3Km

To Shillelagh 2.6Km

150

The route de-tours around wooded Urelands Hill giving occasional views of the Blackstairs Mountains to the south-west, while 27km to the north the slopes of the western outlier of the Wicklow range, Keadeen Mountain, can be seen. There is a pleasant informality about the forestry here, which consists of a mixture of deciduous and coniferous trees, with the odd clump of rhododendron in between, and no regimented pattern in the planting can be discerned. The mixture of trees seems to encourage a rich and melodious birdlife, and in early summer the road margins are decorated with violets, wild strawberries, wood anemones and bluebells.

As the road descends again, Urelands House, an early 19th century stone-built farmhouse, is passed. One of the outbuildings has a gable belfry, which was used in earlier times to call the labourers in the fields to their meals.

The townland to the left of the road is called Burrow, which suggests that a few centuries ago there was a rabbit warren here, where rabbits were bred in great numbers for food and fur. As rabbits were introduced into Ireland by the Normans, the name is a relatively new one, and the only non-Gaelic name in the area.

The route crosses a stream into county Carlow at Wicklow Bridge. A little further south, the stream is joined by the Derry river, after which the opposite bank of the river is in county Wexford. The name Derry comes from the Gaelic for 'oak', and harks back to the time when great oakwoods blanketed this area. Wicklow oak was well known throughout Britain and Ireland for its strength and resistance to rot, and the Norman King William Rufus requested it to be used in the construction of Westminister Hall in London in the 11th century. In subsequent centuries, the majority of the timber went towards the construction of the English Navy; it was reported in 1608 that Shillelagh had sufficient oak to keep the navy supplied with ships for 20 years.

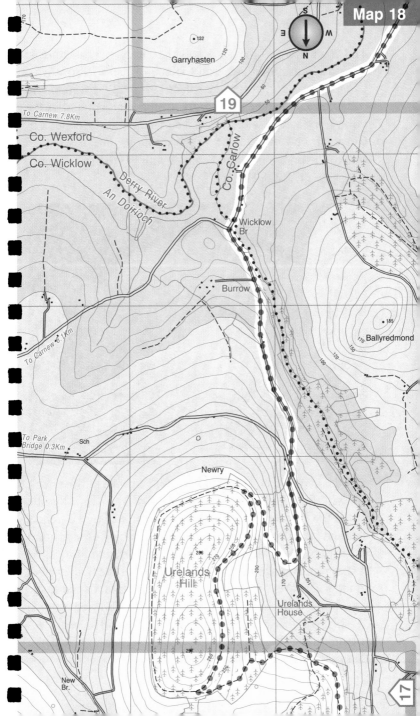

Map 18

Garryhasten

• 132

To Carnew 7.8Km

Co. Wexford

Co. Wicklow

Derry River
An Doirioch

Co. Carlow

Wicklow
Br

Burrow

• 185

Ballyredmond

To Carnew 6.1Km

To Park
Bridge 0.3Km

Sch

Newry

Urelands
Hill

286

Urelands
House

297

New
Br.

19

17

The route follows the road and the Derry river south-east towards Clonegal village and the end of the Wicklow Way. Clonegal is a picturesque place of late Georgian and Victorian houses and shopfronts. At the southern end of the village is a bridge with a plaque commemorating the men of Clonegal who died in the 1798 rebellion, on the Wexford side of the bridge is a small hamlet with the romantic sounding name of Watch House.

Huntington Castle

Off the main street, at the end of a long avenue of lime trees, you will find Huntington Castle. Originally a typical castle of the towerhouse type, it was erected in 1625 by Laurence, 1st (and last) Lord Esmonde. His job was to oversee the timber harvesting in the area, and the transportation of logs, by floating them down the Derry river, and via the Slaney river to the sea at Wexford. Over succeeding centuries the castle was much extended, re-modeled and modernised (in the 1880s it was the second private house in Ireland to have electric lighting installed), the result being the charming mansion that graces Clonegal today.

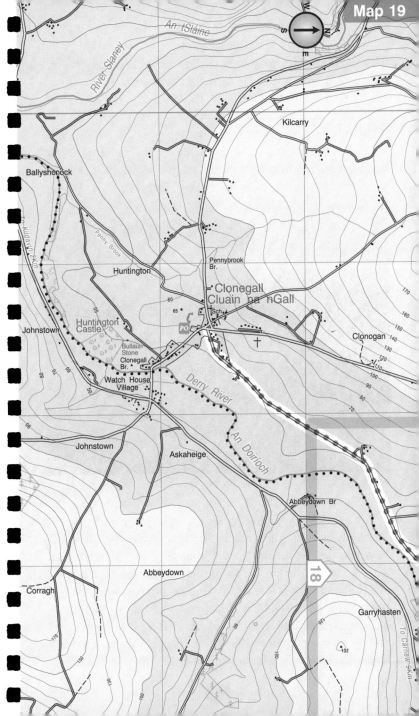

Map 19

An tSláine

River Slaney

Kilcarry

Ballyshonock

Penny Brook

Kildavin 2km

Huntington

Pennybrook Br.

Clonegall
Cluain na nGall

Sch

60

65

PO

Johnstown

Huntington Castle

Clonogan

140

150

160

170

130

120

110

100

90

80

70

Bullaun Stone

Clonegall Br.

Watch House Village

Derry River

An Doiríoch

Johnstown

Askaheige

Abbeydown Br

18

Abbeydown

Corragh

Garryhasten

To Carnew 9km

132

170

150

60

100

Glendalough

The Wicklow Way passes through many dramatically scenic places as it wends it's way through the mountains, but probably the most impressive is Glendalough. Thousands of years ago, a great glacier worked its way eastwards from the highlands, grinding and carving out the typical U shaped valley that is Glendalough today. As the ice sheet melted, it left behind a place of great beauty, a long, dark lake fed by two mountain streams, overlooked by forest-clad towering heights.

Glendalough

In the 6th century AD St Kevin is said to have come upon the valley seeking quietude in which to spend a life of meditation. He founded a monastery here, 'where two clear rivers flow together', probably at the joining of the Glenealo and the Glendasan, where the present cluster of ruined churches and the round tower stand. Leaving his monks to run the settlement he had established, Kevin withdrew up the valley and established a hermitage, where he is said to have spent much of the remainder of his life in prayer. There are many legends about his asceticism, and his love of animals.

Legends tell of wild beasts coming to drink water from his hand; on one occasion he is said to have stood in the freezing lake with his arms outstretched for so long that a blackbird came and made a nest in his cupped hand, and he remained until the young were hatched.

After Kevin's death Glendalough attracted many pilgrims, and in time the modest settlement founded by him became a monastic city and a great centre of religion and learning. Many of the buildings of the 'city' were timber built, and even the important stone buildings originally had timber roofs covered in thatch, so fire was a frequent problem.

The place was first destroyed by fire in 770 AD, and over the next four hundred years Glendalough was burned, plundered or destroyed on twenty separate occasions, including nine times by the Vikings, who began to carry out raids on Ireland about 795 AD.

At its most powerful, even the Norse town of Dublin came under the ecclesiastical jurisdiction of Glendalough, but on the coming of the Normans, the roles were reversed. The importance of Dublin diocese increased and eventually Glendalough became annexed to it. The monastery gradually waned, and with all other monasteries in Ireland was suppressed in the 16th century.

Pilgrimages, however, continued, and the numbers attending the 'Pattern' on the saints day, June 3rd, increased dramatically in the 19th century. It also became a venue for inter-clan faction fights. William Wilde, father of Oscar, writing in 1873, described a 'Pattern' he attended in his youth, and how, as the processing and praying gradually came to an end, the music, dancing and drunken brawls began!

Today, peace has returned again to Glendalough, drawing

processions of visitors to its beautiful ruins and the silent lacustrine valley that attracted St Kevin so long ago.

A Brief Description of the Monastic Remains

The Entrance Gateway: The monastic area is entered through the remains of a gatehouse, which would originally have had an upper storey occupied by the custodian of the gate. Monasteries were not subject to secular laws, and any fugitive who gained entrance to a monastery such as this was given safe sanctuary from the outside world.

Round Tower

The Tower: Rising more than 30m from the centre of the graveyard is Glendalough's round tower, a unique Irish building type, and a symbol of Ireland's Middle-Ages reputation as the Island of Saints and Scholars.

These dramatic buildings had a number of purposes, but served mainly as bell towers and places of safety when the monastery was under attack. Glendalough was attacked by the Vikings in 833 AD and 835 AD, and fifty years later they were back again.

During this period, when it became clear that all monasteries were vulnerable, round towers were constructed to confront the threat. When warning of a attack was received, the settlement would be evacuated, with messen- gers hurrying to seek assistance from the nearest friendly clan. Any valuables which were not easily portable were taken up into the tower by a small group of monks, who then pulled up the access ladder after them and bolted the door, four metres above ground level. One can imagine the pale frightened faces peering out of the narrow windows at the rampaging Norsemen below. The invaders probably had lit- tle time to try to smoke or burn the monks out of their hide- away before they would have had to flee back to the coast when reinforcements arrived.

Celtic High Cross

The Cathedral: This is the largest of the seven churches of Glendalough, and it occupies a central position in the monastic settlement. The building you see today is probably the 9th century replacement for a timber building that was burnt in 833 AD, and completely destroyed in 835 AD, which was itself plundered in 886 AD and 977 AD. It ceased to be a cathedral in 1214, when Glendalough was absorbed into the Dublin diocese. It consists of three main areas, the nave, the chancel and a small sacristy off the chancel, and displays some very beautiful decorative stone carving. The walls are lined inside with grave slabs, the dates of which range over a thousand years from the 9th to the 19th century.

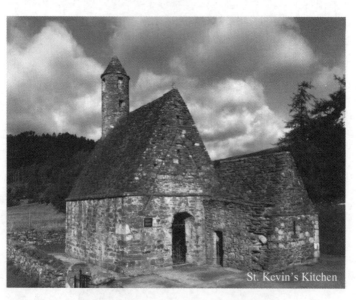

St. Kevin's Kitchen

St Kevins Kitchen: This is the stone-roofed church with the mini-round tower on its roof, downhill from the cathedral, probably dating from the 8th or 9th century. It is the most complete building in Glendalough, probably saved by virtue of it's unburnable vaulted roof, which allowed it to be used again as a church for a period in the early 19th century. Beam holes in the walls indicate it once had an upper floor, four metres above the ground floor, which may have been living quarters or possibly a repository for manuscripts.

The Spink

Upper Glendalough

There is much of interest in the immediate environs of the valley to keep one occupied for some days. In particular, the valley beyond the Upper Lake is well worth a visit: there and back is about 7Km. It is a place of ice-carved cliffs, scree slopes and waterfalls, where red deer and feral goats roam and graze, and ravens and peregrine falcons quarter the skies.

At the Upper Lake follow the road through the trees along the northern shore. The road was built to access the mines in the upper reaches of the valley in the early 1800s. Across the lake an oakwood can be seen clinging to the steep cliffs; these trees are among a few small pockets that represent all that remains of the great oakwoods that once covered Wicklow.

The road emerges from the trees to pass a picturesque sandy beach at the far end of the lake. An interface between the old schist that up to 400 million years ago covered the area, and the newer granite can be seen in the cliffs to the right; heather grows easily in the old soft schist, but dislikes the bare hard granite, so where the heather ends is where the granite takes over.

Soon the old mine workings, rising out of a sea of white powdered quartz, are reached. Lead ore was mined here from the early 1800s to about 1920, and at one time over a hundred miners lived and worked in the valley. The white quartz scars on the landscape will remain for many years because the arsenic from the lead ore prevents any plant growth.

Upper Lake

Farther on, at the far side of the river, you may spot a herd of feral goats, great, shaggy long-coated animals with curling horns. There is a herd of about eighty of these animals, descendants of domestic goats that long ago escaped into the wild, in the valley.

A squealing sound high in the air may be the first sign that a peregrine falcon, Ireland's largest raptor, is about. They nest on ledges in the towering cliffs here, and prey on pigeons and smaller birds.

Beyond the mines a zig-zag mule track leads up beside the cascading Glenealo river into a little-frequented higher valley, called Van Diemen's Land. In this upper valley look out for red deer; a large herd grazes in this area, and you may spot does and their young on the higher ground. There are also badgers and Irish mountain hares in the area, but all you may want to do after climbing to this view-point is to recline on the pavements beside the river and look back over Glendalough, or even have a swim in one of the many inviting pools - and who could blame you!

Pool in Glendalough

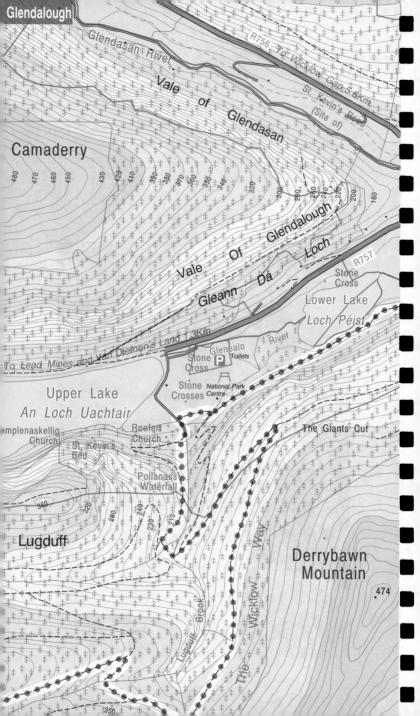

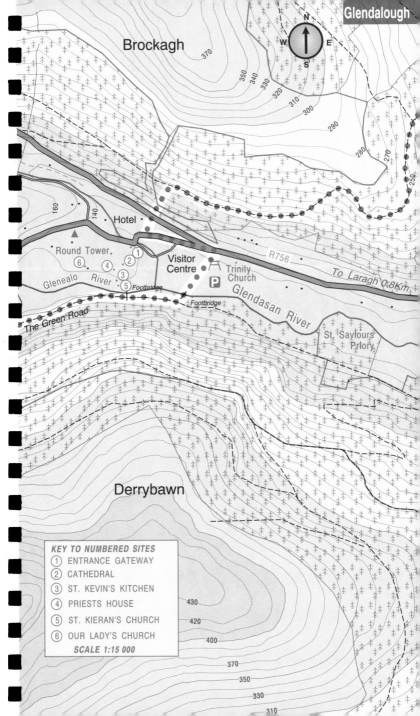

Glendalough

Brockagh

N
W E
S

Hotel

Round Tower

⑥ ④ ②①

⑤ Footbridge

③

Visitor Centre

Trinity Church

P

Glenealo River

The Green Road

Footbridge

R756

Glendasan River

To Laragh 0.8Km

St. Saviours Priory

Derrybawn

KEY TO NUMBERED SITES
① ENTRANCE GATEWAY
② CATHEDRAL
③ ST. KEVIN'S KITCHEN
④ PRIESTS HOUSE
⑤ ST. KIERAN'S CHURCH
⑥ OUR LADY'S CHURCH
SCALE 1:15 000

Notes